Observations on American Architecture

by

Ivan Chermayeff

with photographs

by Elliott Erwitt

NA
705
.C43

Text Copyright 1972 in all countries of the International Copyright
Union by Ivan Chermayeff
Photographs Copyright 1972 in all countries of the International Copyright
Union by Elliott Erwitt
All rights reserved
First published in 1972 by The Viking Press, Inc.
625 Madison Avenue, New York, N. Y. 10022
Published simultaneously in Canada by
The Macmillan Company of Canada Limited
SBN 670-52019-5
Library of Congress catalog card number: 72-81663
Printed and bound in Japan

Dabney Lancaster Library
Longwood College
Farmville, Virginia

Observations on American Architecture

by
Ivan Chermayeff
with
photographs
by
Elliott Erwitt

73-03629

The Viking Press
New York
1972

Acknowledgments

This book began in the United States Pavilion at the World Exposition held in Osaka, Japan. Included in the pavilion among other exhibitions was one entitled Architecture: U. S. A., in which approximately one hundred buildings were presented to the Japanese people. Most of the buildings in that exhibition are included here, although some have been eliminated because they were very specifically selected for a Japanese audience, others because I changed my mind about them in the present context. Many more have been added since.

The U. S. Pavilion was conceived and designed in its entirety by a team of architects and designers with the unwieldy name of Davis, Brody, Chermayeff, Geismar, de Harak Associates. For their encouragement to me in my development of the concept of the architectural exhibition, I thank my architect partners in the U. S. Pavilion project, Lewis Davis and Samuel Brody, as well as designer Rudolph de Harak. Even more, my partner of many years, Tom Geismar, for his patience and understanding during those months and the many months afterward required to reorganize the exhibition material into this book.

The United States Information Agency was responsible for the U. S. participation in Expo '70 and consequently for the approval of this particular project. The support of Jack Masey, USIA Director of Design, was essential to the exhibition and greatly appreciated. I am also indebted to Peter Blake, editor of *Architectural Forum*, Stephen Kliment, then editor of *Architectural & Engineering News*, and Arthur Drexler of the Museum of Modern Art for their suggestions of contemporary buildings. Along with the late Sybil Moholy-Nagy, these friends contributed to the list of buildings from which I selected the Osaka exhibition.

Conversations with many architects have been most valuable, especially those with my father, Serge Chermayeff, and my brother, Peter, whose good advice and sharp objective eyes have helped me. Most of the other architects with whom I have talked and whose work I know and admire are represented in these pages with projects that speak for themselves.

Mrs. Charles Kuskin gave me considerable help ordering my loose thoughts and the book itself.

Most of all, I would like to thank my collaborator, Elliott Erwitt, for the care and understanding he has taken in photographing the buildings all over the United States. His unfailing eye and brilliant pictures have put the work of many architects in a light which I hope they will find sympathetic. I.C.

Preface

It is much easier to describe what this book is not about than to try to explain what it is about. Certainly it is neither an historical survey nor a scholarly approach.

It is instead the presentation of personal feelings and observations about the forms of architecture as they exist in the United States. The buildings selected are all distinguished, at least in their appearance. Some are old, dating back to pre-Revolutionary or Revolutionary days, others to the pre-Victorian era or to World War I. They are intentionally mixed with the best contemporary architecture, predominantly that of the late 1960s.

Seeing buildings that have been designed by carpenters or perhaps politicians of earlier times side by side with contemporary, sometimes fashionable, architecture clarifies the fundamental similarities between many of them. This juxtaposition illustrates aesthetically that there is very little new in the world. Certainly it is the timeless aspects of architecture that are important and also most interesting. The finest contemporary work, unless it is purely technological, will always be found to be strongly rooted in design of the past.

As soon as we refrain from arranging buildings chronologically, those a century and a half old become as contemporary as their "modern" counterparts. Looked at in this way, these structures appear as parts of a whole rather than consecutive steps along the historic path of architectural design.

The finest work will never be dated. It will always remain excellent, although it may not always be popular. But popularity is a poor gauge for anything as permanent or commanding as a building. Architecture as we see it in the Sunday newspaper rotogravure sections, house and garden magazines, and even the professional journals is usually a presentation of prize-winning fashions. The best of such works, always the least in number, use their heritage of basic design elements with the most strength. More commonly, however, we are presented with a collection of fashion plates which are no more or less interesting than that term implies. The fact that fashion is a transitory concept and building is not makes the two poor companions. While last January's *Harper's Bazaar* is a dead issue by February, such unaptly named apartment houses as the Renoir and the Picasso on Manhattan's East Side will not disappear as quickly or as inexpensively.

Those buildings that grow logically out of the materials from which they are fabricated and let that logic penetrate clearly to the onlooker are truly satisfying. The barns, silos, and outbuildings of the American farm landscape in assorted woods, stones, or a combination of both are an endless wonder. The traditional Cape Cod and colonial wood-frame structures are a triumph of quality over expediency.

In choosing buildings for this book, I have had to ignore, for reasons of space, the vast middle ground of buildings erected between the two world wars together with some of the best postwar architecture. The new office buildings of major corporations and institutions built during the fifties and early sixties have been well-documented elsewhere. For this reason Connecticut General Life Insurance in Hartford, Pepsi-Cola, Lever House, Chase Manhattan Bank, and CBS, all in New York, the Lake Shore apartments of Mies van der Rohe in Chicago, and many other buildings which sprang up in San Francisco, Dallas, and most other large American cities, are not included, even though they are certainly as great as many of the buildings that followed them in the mid 1960s.

This book does also not include some of the very important new structures that have been made possible by technological advances. There are beautiful, intricate, and inventive structures that have emerged from projects involved with offshore oil drilling or the Apollo program, such as the floating rigs out in the Gulf of Mexico or the gantry for the Saturn V rockets at Cape Kennedy. To include nonarchitected structures in this book, however, would suggest a broader definition of architecture than is intended here. The purer such structures are, the less they have to do with architects and the more with engineers. R. Buckminster Fuller's domes are the perfect example. Their forms are the result of programs and calculations without artistic overtones of any kind. One can rely on the fact that structures that are simply honest expressions of their intent, such as the gantries and bridges, have enormous aesthetic value. A sense of satisfaction is always gained from seeing a structure that suggests that it really performs the way it was meant to.

There is a great difference between looking at architecture and living with it. For the observer a building appears ugly or beautiful according to one's particular taste. But a building that you work or live in is not only felt differently; it is eventually seen differently. Feeling changes seeing. An "ugly" building that really works can become aesthetically rewarding, just as a "beautiful" building that does not work will rapidly lose its looks. The image of the pretty face fades as the basic inadequacies are revealed and their permanence grows glaringly visible.

Many buildings, and no doubt some in this book, are basically intriguing pieces of sculpture. For those who are not threatened with having to pass many days in them they are almost redeemable on these grounds. Had these buildings been allowed to remain unheated and unoccupied, preferably in an open field somewhere, with no program or purpose attached to them, they might be even purer sculpture. Such buildings, of course, would be considerably cheaper constructed without ducts, plumbing, and plate glass.

It is probable that a number of buildings appearing on these pages may not even fulfill that one fundamental criterion: a building must work. This is not to say that "form must follow function." Function can have a much greater scope than mere utility and economy. It can certainly include such qualities as grandeur, dramatic gesture, extravagant materials, when the purposes of the building justify such expressions. If, however, as is so often the case, the avowed purposes of the building are ignored or rationalized, then the final result becomes an irresponsible act that is difficult to pardon.

In the past architecture was legitimately thought of as the "Mother of the Arts." From the earliest monumental buildings through the Classic Period, the Middle Ages, and the Renaissance, architecture encompassed painting and sculpture. There was, in fact, little separation between the arts. Pericles was a sculptor as well as an architect, and Bernini was an architect as well as a sculptor.

During the seventeenth and eighteenth centuries architects and patrons alike were members of the creative and sophisticated elite, striving for and demanding excellence. Distinguished architects were employed to give permanent stature and focus to a religious or social function, make a vista, or determine the character of a city square. This desire still exists, but present circumstances make such achievements almost impossible. The role of architecture has changed, although only the best architects realize this and they don't necessarily act as if they had the knowledge in hand. In today's world planning has become that subject or profession at the core of society's needs, superseding architecture and relegating it to the class of a luxury. Today one building of quality, plus or minus, makes far less impact on the urban environment than it used to. In many ways the accumulation of good buildings, unrelated to each other, in fact competing with each other, is not as great a contribution to a city as tearing some of these private and excellent buildings down would be and, instead, providing meeting places for people. Considering the magnetism building sites have for pedestrians, even a hole in the ground could be preferable to the addition of another building, no matter how distinguished the building and how undistinguished the hole. Despite these feelings there are no illustrations of holes in the ground in the following pages.

The motivation for selecting buildings throughout this book is fundamentally aesthetic, not historical. Therefore the basic design elements of form, texture, line, structure, light, and shadow as they apply to any building, old or new, are more important than their particular place in the history of American architecture. For this reason, some of the buildings included have anonymous architects, while the works of other very renowned architects have not been included.

The form that buildings take can frequently be recognized as leaning very strongly, often too far, overboard in one aesthetic direction. To put it another way, the initial design impetus is highly motivated and often prejudiced. Architects or, traditionally, builders have always wanted their buildings to be a noteworthy expression.

The most obvious expression is one that takes advantage of a dramatic gesture. The spire of a church, surpassing the lower buildings around it, reaches into the sky and becomes awesome. Such a strong sense of direction in a building demands attention because it combines a powerful form with the force of the idea that motivated it. At various points in history gesture in architecture has been channeled into style. Angular shedlike roofs, establishing a single strong visual direction, or many angular forms flying off in all directions, have been employed across the country. The shed-roof was in vogue in the 1950s until all the best architects sensed that the newness had gone out of it and that something else would have to be tried. The most successful and best-known architects have an instinct for knowing when an innovation is about to become a boring cliché and when what was a boring cliché can be introduced once more as an innovation.

When a style is too widely adopted, it becomes banal. Like a field, however, a successful architectural style needs to lie fallow after a good crop. This by no means suggests that the field no longer has value. Its time will come again.

Shedlike, angular roofs returned to vogue once more, among the bright young architects, during the late 1960s. In fact, 1970 has been described in architectural circles as "The Year of the Shed." When an angular roof lets the north light into a studio space, keeps the snow from piling up, or otherwise responds to a special need, the results are particularly gratifying, although that may not have been the architect's original intention.

Architectural form of a predominantly simple and solid nature, rooted to the ground, is perhaps the most difficult to design with real distinction. Buildings that are successfully developed from the simplest geometric forms—cubes, cones, pyramids—can be the most inspiring kind of architecture. They are least faddish and most timeless. Barns, round and rectangular, and the wood and stone silos, in all their varieties throughout the United States, are almost always extraordinarily pleasing and have been widespread in their influence.

In a desire to create monuments architects often become infatuated with a single overriding concept. The St. Louis arch, for instance, with its more than six hundred feet of height and its interior elevators, is acceptable on aesthetic grounds because of its size. The arch reduced to desk-top size, as it is in every St. Louis gift shop, is ludicrous, if not actually ugly. This disease, which great architects are particularly prone to, could be called the King Kong Syndrome. In other words, if your design is somewhat questionable, make it big enough and it will be impressive. Without his size King Kong would have been just another monkey.

Another unusually common architectural malady can be described as the Marble Halls Complex. When the opportunity for exaggerated size cannot be rationalized, a desire to use extraordinarily expensive materials as the steppingstones to greatness takes over. Unfortunately, travertine doesn't automatically make great space, and Cor-ten steel's instant patina does not include a guarantee of character.

Any list of truly good architects, in the sense of imaginative, talented, responsible, and contributing (more than interesting or merely influential) is either much too long or much too short. In the front ranks of a short list beside the masters, Mies, Saarinen, and Neutra, must stand José Luis Sert, Louis Kahn, Kevin Roche, Marcel Breuer, and I. M. Pei, all of whom have mastered more than once the ingredients, particularly form, that go into the making of great architecture.

It is interesting to note that each of the great architects mentioned above brings to the mind of anyone slightly familiar with their work a hazy but nevertheless recognizable architectural image. Each of these architects has had the talent to find his own strengths, describe and nurture his own tastes, develop his own architectural language, and, above all, to get that which he had envisioned built. Every one of these architects has had the extraordinary energy necessary to accomplish a large measure of what he set out to do.

Among all of America's best contemporary architects, there exist certain design tendencies, visual themes from which each individual produces both his most as well as his least consequential work. A mutant offspring or distortion of the norm brings forth the triumphs as well as the disasters, depending largely on the quality of rationalization that has taken place about each individual project.

Out of a real devotion to the capabilities of steel and glass technology Mies van der Rohe developed a level of quality that he expressed through proportion and detail almost never equaled by others.

As Mies himself put it: "God is in the details." Few other architects, and there are thousands who are basically his aesthetic descendants, have either the discipline or the intensity required to match his performance.

Like the painter Josef Albers, Mies finally restricted himself to the simplest and most exquisite vocabulary. In the series of paintings and prints "Homage to the Square," Albers has committed himself like a tireless laboratory researcher. The square is a workable format for his experiments in color. The format gives Albers the freedom to devote himself solely to his interest in color without other distractions. The results of this seemingly microscopic view finally describe a whole world. Mies was, in this sense, a tireless scientist, too.

Eero Saarinen, rather than perfecting any single style of his own, always seemed to approach each architectural project as though nothing like it had ever existed before. For him God was not in the details. His enormous energies were dedicated to a search for a quintessential architectural concept which would appropriately symbolize, in form at least, some aspect of its function. Or if the building could not specifically become a visual image of his client's activities, it could at the very least exploit some new technological capability in architectural construction. Other Saarinen buildings were new variations of more conventional architectural solutions.

The Saarinen office produced the brilliant General Motors Complex in Detroit. This is fundamentally an International Style group of buildings utilizing the most advanced construction technology available for the windows: a neoprene gasketing technique until then unexplored.

Saarinen's other work, designed and built during the postwar years, unlike the production of other architectural offices, can usually be thought of and described in reference to some basic form, either mathematical or highly technological, or even as purely romantic in origin.

In essence, Saarinen's last major building, CBS headquarters in New York, was the result of two very basic aesthetic notions. The first was that a rectangular office building, fully utilizing the volume allowed by the New York City building codes, need not be yet another variation of the steel and glass box, no matter how distinguished. The second notion was that such a building could dispense with the normal two-story entrance lobby with its usual canopies. The result, no longer adhering to the accepted formula, is a severely articulated stone façade which sits very dramatically on its site just below street level and which is uninterrupted by the normal, clearly defined commonplace of a supposedly inspiring lobby. Along with the masterfully detailed buildings of Mies van der Rohe, CBS is probably the most distinguished modern office building in New York or any other American city.

Saarinen's love of making projects, bending a situation to make it fulfill a notion or express a yet unexploited form, is apparent in many of his works. With the benefit of hindsight, I can look back to a wartime summer day on Cape Cod as symbolic of Saarinen's approach to problems and indicative of his fantastic energy. Saarinen, disinclined to lying in the sun, decided on a day's project which I, as a small boy, was enlisted for. The project consisted of making a contour map of the bottom of the ten-acre pond in front of our summer cottage. In order to accomplish this task, I rowed Saarinen in a carefully determined grid pattern back and forth across the pond while he dove off the stern of our rowboat at regular intervals with a big stone attached to a rope on one arm. In this way, the depths were measured, each dive taking Saarinen to the bottom of the pond. The stone would most certainly have reached the bottom alone, but for some reason Saarinen felt it necessary to accompany it. Perhaps he wished to be assured firsthand of the bottom's condition; more likely, I suppose, he wanted exercise. At the end of the day the results were charted and a very accurate contour map was drawn up which proved for one thing that the pond was much shallower than anyone who just swam in it had previously guessed.

Saarinen, of all America's contemporary architects, was concerned with basic form and its essence. His associate and successor, Kevin Roche, whose firm completed the Saarinen office projects after his death, has continued with great success to apply his own deep concerns to all the fundamental elements of architectural handwriting—texture, material, line, as well as form. Roche has time and time again demonstrated his mastery of the elements making up the architectural whole. The Oakland Museum alone should qualify as one of the most brilliant architectural achievements of recent times. (See page 110.)

In the same way that Albers serves as a metaphorical comparison to Mies, Mondrian can be used to describe Richard Neutra, whose California houses of the 1930s and 1940s were very pure compositions of lines and planes. Of all contemporary artists, Mondrian looks easiest to copy stylistically. In fact, he is not. Witness how little painting there is that even attempts to imitate his apparently simple arrangements of black lines and primary colors. No painter of equal stature has followed in Mondrian's footsteps. Many of Neutra's houses give one the feeling that the depth of each beam and the length of each wall are perfect and that if any element were either shorter or thinner the building would no longer be harmonious. The "rightness" of Neutra and Mondrian is perhaps a little cold and inhuman. Nonetheless their works are exquisite. (See page 126.)

Marcel Breuer's houses are not exquisite at all. They are strong, earthy, rich with textures and contrasts of light and shadow, and very human indeed. They never make you feel that you should be wearing a tuxedo to enter. Neither does one feel a sense of guilt when something is spilled. These houses are not delicate. They are warm, extremely livable, and quite capable of retaining their own personalities without overawing or smothering the personalities of their inhabitants. The Stillman House (see page 49) is one of the best examples of a Breuer house. Like Breuer himself, the house is like a bear, simple, powerful, and yet not altogether predictable.

Houses, certainly more than office buildings, seem to be an outlet for architects' best expressions. As difficult as it is to design a distinguished contemporary house, it is even more difficult to try to sell one secondhand at anywhere near its original cost. A common understanding or even acceptance of contemporary architecture does not exist. Designing original houses is unprofitable, according to almost all architects, and generally unrewarding in most other terms as well. One loses friends, if not wives or husbands, in the aftermath of housebuilding. Evidently the experience is such a personal, emotional one that it is too traumatic for the average homeowner and/or architect. Perhaps it is this extremely personal involvement that makes private houses so fundamentally interesting to study.

Eliot Noyes, Paul Rudolph, Edward Larrabee Barnes, Harry Weese, Ulrich Franzen, John Johansen, Richard Meier, and Craig Ellwood, among others, have all designed exceptionally satisfactory houses. They have also designed some of the best contemporary architecture in the United States.

Several post-World War II American houses seem to have set the standards for modern architecture around the world. Most significant, perhaps, is Frank Lloyd Wright's house for Edgar Kaufmann, Jr., "Falling Waters," built in Pennsylvania, outside Pittsburgh. It would appear that this house was designed to prove that Wright could create in the International Style better than anyone else. The house is always photographed from below (see page 126) with its cantilevered balconies perched above a waterfall. This single view has influenced more modern architects than the pyramids.

Mies van der Rohe's house for Dr. Edith Farnsworth, outside Chicago, and Philip Johnson's own glass house in New Canaan, Connecticut, are both landmarks of equal stature and notoriety for which other architects will always be indebted. Richard Neutra's "Desert House" in California, built in 1946, ranks with them, even if he said so himself.

Except for the Kaufmann house, none of the above is shown in this book as they do not fall within its limited scope. They are mentioned here because they are great. Many of the houses, designed by talented younger architects, that are shown on the following pages probably never would have been designed without the prior existence of these particular benchmarks.

Ninety per cent of the houses built in the United States are put up by builders or developers who do so without the services of architects. As the industrial age eliminated artists from the scene, architects became obsolete. Consequently, even if builders did not ignore architects, houses would still in the main be plunked mindlessly down on bulldozed and therefore treeless plots, the spaces between them wasted, their picture windows confronting the traffic, and their usable backyard spaces remaining dusty and ignored. The front door always faces the never-viewed, unsafe-for-children lawn with its cast-iron dwarfs and mirrored crystal ball. The aluminum kitchen door is the real entrance, being nearest the car. The front door is used only by mistake, as intimate friends enter by the kitchen too. Any changes from these norms require creative architects. But builders and developers don't use architects because they slow up the bulldozers and increase the costs.

The texture of exterior surfaces in buildings becomes extremely important and often the motivating force in design as soon as a real choice of material and surface treatment becomes available to architects. Initially clapboards, shingles, roughstone, and masonry, plus a few variations in each category, were available. When a substantial difference between buildings was desired, it had to be accomplished by other means of expression.

Cast-iron components, developed at the end of the nineteenth century, brought forth a variety of patterns and designs that were built into the cast-iron components themselves. In much the same way, poured concrete was recognized as an aesthetically acceptable, if not actually desirable, material, as well as a practical one. As Le Corbusier and his disciples around the world gave concrete its aesthetic credentials, so Mies van der Rohe completely legitimized steel and glass. In recent years the potentials of texture as the prominent and even overriding aspect of any given architectural project have been exploited very successfully many times.

The notion of texture as a primary driving force behind architecture takes many forms. The most obvious is the use of rough and raw material. The most subtle is the hard and smooth surfaces of glass and steel, where reflection becomes part of texture.

As I have explained, this book is a menu of personal choices. While it recognizes many architectural staples that have been prepared with grace and talent, it also includes a number of baked Alaskas, parfaits, napoleons, blancmanges, crepes suzette, and other extravaganzas.

There are probably dozens of buildings that could be added or substituted for the new buildings included here. There are perhaps hundreds that could be substituted for the old buildings with which they are interspersed. Every architect will find omissions in his own personal clip file of contemporary work and may also prefer to substitute favorite "architecture without architects," to borrow critic Bernard Rudofsky's phrase. My choices have been limited by time and space as well as preference.

Even as this preface is being written, the press and my own observations bring evidence of new architectural vitality which I wish I could have presented in this book. For instance, an exciting approach to color and structural methods has been taken by John Johansen in his Mummers' Theater Complex in Oklahoma City. This building exemplifies a successful rearrangement of ordinary architectural values and priorities.

Through architectural history it is the continual rediscovery, reevaluation, and reassessment of the design vocabulary that, I believe, is always at the foundation of architectural excellence and progress. It is that mingling of the past and its influences upon the present that I have attempted to show here.

List of Illustrations

Page 49
Stillman Residence
Marcel Breuer and Associates, 1965
Litchfield, Connecticut

Page 50
Pueblo Indian Dwelling
Architect unknown, 17th century
Acoma, New Mexico

Page 51
Bloedel Residence
Ulrich Franzen & Associates, 1965
South Williamstown, Massachusetts

Page 52
Confederate Memorial Chapel
Architect unknown, 1887
Richmond, Virginia

Page 52
Residence
Richard Meier & Associates, 1969
Easthampton, New York

Page 53
Old Humpback Bridge
Architect unknown, c. 1840
Covington, Virginia

Page 54
Catholic Church
Architect unknown, 17th century
Taos, New Mexico

Page 55
Everson Museum of Art, Syracuse University
I. M. Pei & Partners, 1969
Syracuse, New York

Page 56
Silos
Architect unknown, c. 1910 (destroyed 1971)
Saw Mill River Parkway, New York

Page 57
Flatiron Building
Daniel H. Burnham & Company, 1901–1903
New York, New York

Page 57
Knights of Columbus Building
Kevin Roche, John Dinkeloo and Associates, 1968
New Haven, Connecticut

Page 58
Catholic Church
Architect unknown, 17th century
Taos, New Mexico

Page 59
"Stratford," Thomas Lee Residence
Architect unknown, c. 1725
Westmoreland County, Virginia

Page 60
Westyard Office/Warehouse
Davis, Brody & Associates, 1968
New York, New York

Page 61
Hillsboro Hosiery Mill
Architect unknown, c. 1880
Hillsboro, New Hampshire

Page 62
National Center for Atmospheric Research
I. M. Pei & Partners, 1967
Boulder, Colorado

Page 64
Goddard Library, Clark University
John M. Johansen & Associates, 1969
Worcester, Massachusetts

Page 65
Coal Elevator
Architect unknown, c. 1840
Bennington, Vermont

Page 66
Reverend Henry Whitfield Stone House
Architect unknown, 1639
Guilford, Connecticut

Page 66
Morris Mechanic Theatre, Charles Center
John M. Johansen & Associates, 1967
Baltimore, Maryland

Page 67
Walker Sisters' House
Architect unknown, c. 1770
Greenbrier, Tennessee

Page 67
Southside Junior High School
Eliot Noyes & Associates, 1968
Columbus, Indiana

Page 68
Southeastern Massachusetts Technological Institute
Paul Rudolph, 1966
North Dartmouth, Massachusetts

Page 69
Creative Arts Center, Colgate University
Paul Rudolph, 1967
Hamilton, New York

Page 70
Southeastern Massachusetts Technological Institute
Paul Rudolph, 1966
North Dartmouth, Massachusetts

Page 71
City Hall
Kallmann, McKinnell & Knowles, 1969
Boston, Massachusetts

Page 73
Barn
Architect unknown, c. 1850
Pennsylvania

Page 74
Barn
Architect unknown, c. 1850
Pennsylvania

Page 74
Los Angeles International Airport Post Office
Cesar Pelli, 1969
Los Angeles, California

Page 75
Badger Iron Warehouse
Architect unknown, c. 1880
Watervliet, New York

Page 76
Cobblestone Church
Architect unknown, c. 1860
Childs, New York

Page 77
Cobblestone Schoolhouse
Architect unknown, c. 1860
Childs, New York

Page 78
Scientific Data Systems
Craig Ellwood & Associates, 1969
El Segundo, California

Page 79
Portland Memorial Coliseum
Skidmore, Owings & Merrill, 1961
Portland, Oregon

Page 80
Holyoke Center, Harvard University
Sert, Jackson & Gourley, 1965
Cambridge, Massachusetts

Page 81
College of Environmental Design, University of California at Berkeley
Joseph Esherick, Vernon Demars & Donald Olsen, 1966
Berkeley, California

Page 82
Pjepscot Paper Company
Architect unknown, c. 1880
Topsham, Maine

Page 83
John J. Barton Apartments
Evans Woolen & Associates, 1967
Indianapolis, Indiana

Page 84
Cast-Iron Façade, Broome Street and Broadway
Architect unknown, c. 1850
New York, New York

Page 85
Cast-Iron Façade, Broadway
Architect unknown, c. 1850
New York, New York

Page 86
Sauk's Bridge
Architect unknown, 1854
Adams County, Pennsylvania

Page 87
Alcoa Building
Skidmore, Owings & Merrill, 1968
San Francisco, California

Page 88
Ford Foundation
Kevin Roche, John Dinkeloo and Associates, 1968
New York, New York

Page 89
Town House
Paul Rudolph, 1968
New York, New York

Page 90
Time-Life Building
Harry Weese & Associates, 1971
Chicago, Illinois

Page 91
Lake Point Tower
Schipporeit and Heinrich, 1967
Chicago, Illinois

Page 92 (left)
Tennessee Gas Building
Skidmore, Owings & Merrill, 1969
Houston, Texas

Page 92 (right)
Grace Midland Bank Building
Skidmore, Owings & Merrill, 1970
New York, New York

Page 93
Chicago Civic Center
Skidmore, Owings & Merrill, C. F. Murphy Associates, 1968
Chicago, Illinois

Page 94
U. S. Courthouse and Federal Office Building
Mies van der Rohe, C. F. Murphy Associates, 1965
Chicago, Illinois

Page 97
The Cabildo
Architect unknown, c. 1790
New Orleans, Louisiana

Page 98 (top left)
"Longwood," Samuel Sloan Residence
Samuel Sloan, 1860
Natchez, Mississippi

Page 98 (bottom left)
Jacob Sonnenthiel House
Architect unknown, 1887
Galveston, Texas

Page 98 (top right)
La Prete House (The House of the Turk)
Architect unknown, 1835
New Orleans, Louisiana

Page 98 (bottom right)
Jackson Square, Pontalba Apartments
Architect unknown, c. 1850
New Orleans, Louisiana

Page 99
William Carson House
Joseph & Samuel Newsom, 1885
Eureka, California

Page 100
American Brewery
Architect unknown, c. 1890
Baltimore, Maryland

Page 101
Cloud State Bank
Architect unknown, 1881
McLeansboro, Illinois

Page 102
Baltimore Streets
Architects unknown, c. 1850
Baltimore, Maryland

Page 103
Main Street
Architects unknown, c. 1850
Galena, Illinois

Page 104
Sea Ranch
Moore, Lyndon, Turnbull & Whitaker, 1966
Big Sur, California

Page 105
Shaker Commune Buildings
Architect unknown, early nineteenth century
Hancock, Massachusetts

Page 106
Lake Anne Village Center
Whittlesey, Conklin & Rossant, 1967
Reston, Virginia

Page 107
Louisburg Square, Beacon Hill
Architects unknown, 1830–1840
Boston, Massachusetts

Page 108
University of Virginia Campus
Thomas Jefferson, 1817–1826
Charlottesville, Virginia

Page 109
Deere and Company Administrative Center
Eero Saarinen & Associates, 1965
Moline, Illinois

Page 110
Oakland Museum of Art
Kevin Roche, John Dinkeloo & Associates, 1970
Oakland, California

Page 112
Pomfret School Library
Cambridge Seven Associates, Inc., 1971
Pomfret, Connecticut

Page 113
Wallace Memorial Library, Rochester Institute of Technology
Harry Weese & Associates, 1970
Rochester, New York

Page 113
Julliard School for the Performing Arts
Pietro Belluschi, 1970
New York, New York

Page 114
Exodus House Rehabilitation Center
Smotrich & Platt, 1968
New York, New York

Page 114
College of Science,
Rochester Institute of Technology
Anderson, Beckwith, Haible, 1970
Rochester, New York

Page 115
New England Aquarium
Cambridge Seven Associates, Inc., 1969
Boston, Massachusetts

Page 116
Christian Theological Seminary
Edward Larrabee Barnes, 1965
Indianapolis, Indiana

Page 117
Weston High School
Cambridge Seven Associates, Inc., 1969
Weston, Massachusetts

Page 118
"Rattle and Snap,"
George Polk House
Architect unknown, 1816
Columbia, Tennessee

Page 119
Miles Brewton House
Architect unknown, 1769
Charleston, South Carolina

Page 120
Residence
Architect unknown, 1912
Concord, Massachusetts

Page 122
Dunleith House
Architect unknown, 1847
Natchez, Mississippi

Page 123
Litchfield High School
John M. Johansen & Associates, 1969
Litchfield, Connecticut

Page 124
D'Evereux Mansion
Architect unknown, 1840
Natchez, Mississippi

Page 125
Cummins Technical Center
Harry Weese & Associates, 1970
Columbus, Indiana

Page 126
"Falling Water," Kaufmann House
Frank Lloyd Wright, 1936
Bear Run, Pennsylvania

Page 126
Tremaine House
Richard Neutra, 1949
Montecito, California

Page 127
Pool Residence
James Stewart Polshek, 1969
Sands Point, New York

Page 128
Cleo Rogers Memorial Library
I. M. Pei & Partners, 1968
Columbus, Indiana

Page 129
Noyes Residence
Eliot Noyes, 1956
New Canaan, Connecticut

Page 130
Design Research, Inc.
Benjamin Thompson & Associates, 1970
Cambridge, Massachusetts

Page 132
Crown & Eagle Mill
Architect unknown, c. 1870
North Uxbridge, Massachusetts

Page 133
Factory Buildings
Architect unknown, nineteenth century
Fall River, Massachusetts

Page 134
Chermayeff Residence
Peter Chermayeff, 1970
Concord, Massachusetts

Page 135
Smith Residence
Richard Meier & Associates, 1967
Darien, Connecticut

Page 136
O'Connor Residence
Serge Chermayeff, 1965
Wellfleet, Massachusetts

Page 137
Curry Residence
Richard D. Kaplan, 1970
Montauk Point, New York

Page 138
Alfred Newton Richards Medical Research Building,
University of Pennsylvania
Louis Kahn, 1961
Philadelphia, Pennsylvania

Page 140
Factory Buildings
Architect unknown, 19th century
Fall River, Massachusetts

Page 140
Factory Buildings
Architect unknown, 19th century
Fall River, Massachusetts

Page 142
Married Student Housing,
Harvard University
Sert, Jackson & Gourley, 1967
Cambridge, Massachusetts

Architecture begins with form.
And form begins with gesture.

Defining a vista in Charleston or overpowering Chicago, a thrust into the sky is an awe-inspiring gesture.

A sea of stairs by Thomas Jefferson at the University of Virginia is no less dramatic.

The Spanish Catholic churches of Taos and Trampas, New Mexico, embody the tradition of gesture in religious architecture.

Angular roofs establish a style. Below, in the Whitman House in Connecticut, built in 1660, and left, a house in Illinois, 1802. The contemporary houses at the right date from 1963 and 1970, more than a century and a half later.

The twin bell towers of the New Mexican churches, the stair towers at Cornell University, and the chimneys of the Seward Mansion resemble the gesture of hands held high in the air.

The Courthouse of Cahokia, Illinois, above left, which might be imagined as an early Frank Lloyd Wright house because of its cantilevered flat and jutting roofline, was actually constructed in 1737.

The Cloister in Ephrata, Pennsylvania, was built c. 1743

In spite of the two-hundred-year time span between these American houses, the similarities between them are as great as their differences.

The sheer Arizona canyon wall with its Pueblo cliff dwellings cut into its sides is like the man-made walls of the Rochester Institute, broken only by entrance openings.

The Belle Meade Barn in Tennessee on the previous pages is a magnificent building. Although it is punctuated with a great variety of smaller shapes and forms, each necessary and carefully considered, they never detract from the majesty of the over-all form. Above, the ancestral home of President James K. Polk, also in Tennessee, like a wood-frame Massachusetts house built in 1636, is a compact and sturdy mass. No doubt the scale of both buildings has improved over the years with the growth of adjacent trees.

White clapboard siding accented with perfectly proportioned windows and exquisite details established the highest standards for American architecture at its simplest and best.

HOPE. 7

The Hope #7 firehouse and the Burden Iron Company office, both in Troy, New York, are predominantly expressions of form. They are so powerful and solid that even their great brick arches only add to their solidity.

The varied forms in architect Tom McNulty's own house are harmonious variations in poured concrete. The forms of the Shaker Barn change from round in stone to faceted when logic demanded a wood structure for the second level. Each component, including the fences, in this compound of buildings appears to be a direct response to a clearly understood need. The job each building performs is naturally expressed by its design.

United Daughters of Confederacy
MUSEUM
MAINTAINED BY DONATIONS
• PUBLIC MARKET •
1841

The architectural treatment of the flood-level slave quarters in the Charleston, South Carolina, market building is clearly different from the classic building style above it. The massive stone entrance and foundation walls of Marcel Breuer's Stillman House in Connecticut play against the powerful stucco forms that rest on them. The two distinct visual qualities used in each of the two buildings are in perfect balance.

Square and round forms meet in Acoma, New Mexico, and in New England.

Rectangular shapes and curved lines combine, each accentuating the characteristics of the other.

Even though the Everson Museum and the back of the Taos Church are very different in construction as well as motivation, the similar juxtaposing of great masses elicits a common emotional response.

The four towers of Kevin Roche's building for the Knights of Columbus echo silos in the American landscape. The Flatiron Building, designed by its site, foreshadowed the round building vogue of the 1960s. To date none of the heirs is as satisfactory as the original.

Twin bell towers of this New Mexico church are close in spirit to the widow's walks of the magnificent Virginia residence of Thomas Lee. The extraordinary entrances of both buildings ally them further. On the following pages forms can be seen clearly expressing the functions contained within them.

GRAIN
COAL WOOD
CEMENT SALT LIME
STRAW HAY
GRIST MILL

Occasionally forms become highly articulated exaggerations of their inner activities.

In some cases it appears that form manipulates the original motivating functional requirements.

Forms and forms within forms are brought together masterfully in the brilliant architecture of Paul Rudolph. The sculptural sophistication of his buildings is almost unparalleled. Boston City Hall, at right, designed by Kallmann, McKinnell & Knowles, is also complex in its form. The effect is as handsome as it is difficult to understand in its New England environment.

Texture begins with decoration. All over America bits of color and design motifs have been painted on or attached to the sides of buildings. Very few of these additions are as successful or delightful as Pennsylvania Dutch hex signs and designs.

The exposed and exquisitely detailed columns of Cesar Pelli's Los Angeles International Airport Post Office, while structurally very different, serve the same visual function as the painted door and window frames of old barns.

The classic design motifs of the first cast-iron building panels begin to suggest the use of over-all texture.

Cobblestone buildings of the 1860s in Childs, New York.

Texture is expressed by contrasting surfaces, glass against aggregate, the fabric of mullions between panes, the patterns of window openings, light and shadows playing against columns. External elements, such as trees or reflected images of adjacent buildings, sky, or plants, often become essential aspects of the architectural scheme.

Pronounced architectural detailing makes texture out of light and shadow.

GIN
WHISKEY
WINE
PARKING
CLEANERS
LAUNDRY
DRIVE IN
MASS. AVE. BILLIARDS
Coca-Cola
U-HAUL

New York City's glorious cast-iron
buildings that are, regrettably,
fast disappearing.

COTTON FABRICS
BROADWAY MFRS. SUPPLY CO.
COTTON FABRICS

Structure as texture seen on a covered Pennsylvania bridge and in Alcoa's headquarters in San Francisco.
On the following pages texture is created by elements external to each building. In the Ford Foundation headquarters plants create the architectural surface, while the façade of a New York City private house consists more of reflected buildings than of itself.

NO PARKING
TOW AWAY ZONE
NO PARKING

CULLERTON
YOUR VOTE IS A PRICELESS HERITAGE
JIM BEAM
A family art
for 175 years.

Cor-ten steel and bronzed glass in architect Harry Weese's Time-Life Chicago offices. To the right and below, Mies van der Rohe's curved glass building, originally conceived in 1921 and realized by his disciples in 1967.

In Houston, New York, and Chicago three distinguished office buildings in which texture is created by patterns repeated on an enormous scale. On the next pages Mies's own Federal Office Building stands as the ultimate achievement of perfectly proportioned steel and glass.

The piling of intricate elements, one on top of the other, is the essence of decorative architecture—delightful, rich, and, like wedding cake, to be sampled sparingly. At right, an elegantly proportioned, overdecorated building in New Orleans.

The exuberence of nineteenth-century latticework, wood, and iron balustrades and balconies is seen in the architecture of Natchez, Galveston, and New Orleans. Above, the deliciously absurd mansion of lumber baron William Carson aptly built in Eureka, California, about 1885.

Beer, money, and Victoriana in Baltimore and McLeansboro, Illinois. No possibility for adornment has been overlooked.

BANK
PEOPLES NATIONAL BANK
PEOPLES NATIONAL BANK

Lines and forms, masses and textures carried beyond single houses into the streets of Baltimore and of Galena, Illinois.

WELCOME
TO
GALENA
Miller
HIGH LIFE
Meadow Gold
Meadow Gold
GALENA GAZETTE
MUSEUM & PRINTERY
OAKBRAND
ICE CREAM
EAT

A group of farm buildings that has developed over the years, shed by shed, barn by barn, in response to need and growth, when done with care and craftsmanship, is almost always a greater aesthetic success than a collection of structures that in their total are preconceived and designed. When aesthetics alone are the *raison d'être*, the aesthetic results are almost inevitably less.

The bowfront buildings of Boston's Louisburg Square, like the houses in the new town of Reston, Virginia, have been planned in relation to each other so that they become the meaningful parts of a well-designed whole.

Thomas Jefferson's University of Virginia campus makes full use of the land as an element of the architecture. Architect Eero Saarinen's elegant Japanese-influenced John Deere building is inseparable from its site. On the two pages following is the superb Oakland Museum designed by Saarinen's former associate, Kevin Roche. The project is a series of garden terraces with the interior gallery spaces buried underground beneath them. The greatness of this architecture is experienced more easily than seen.

Massive articulated forms with strong, expressive openings typify the best American architecture of the late 1960s.

Clear definitions of structure, such as the contrasting of exposed concrete and brick or the articulating of window openings and precast panels, add considerably to the quality of form.

New England Aquarium

"Rattle and Snap," Columbia, Tennessee, and a mansion in Charleston. Throughout the United States, particularly during the nineteenth century, the design of many mansions exploited the best traditions of architecture with elegance and style. Their presence has influenced contemporary buildings.

The D'Evereux mansion in Natchez and the Cummins Engine Company building in Indiana with predominantly vertical orientations.

Shown above is "Falling Water," Frank Lloyd Wright's house for Edgar Kaufmann, Jr. Below it is the Tremaine house by Richard Neutra. "Falling Water" is one of three houses by three architects that have influenced innumerable modern architects. Ranking with it are Mies van der Rohe's house for Dr. Edith Farnsworth on the Fox River outside

Chicago and Neutra's famous "Desert House" built in California in 1946. All three houses lie outside the self-imposed limits of this book. However, they are noted here because very few of the excellent houses that followed them would have been possible without their existence. None of them has ever been surpassed.

Form, line, space, and texture are brought together superbly in I. M. Pei's library for Columbus, Indiana, and in architect Eliot Noyes's own house in Connecticut.

An exquisite relationship of mass against open space is achieved for Design Research in Cambridge, Massachusetts. The plate glass is placed directly into the poured concrete floor slabs.

The nineteenth-century factory buildings are possibly the most impressive examples of an architecture bringing together mass, line, texture, and gesture. It is unfortunate that so many have been abandoned and torn down. It seems that all too soon they will be a vanished breed.

Spaces, openings, planes, and volumes punctuated and accented in two elegant contemporary houses.

The sensitive balance of architectural elements, the use of simple materials in these houses, extends into structures of much greater complexity, such as Louis Kahn's Richards laboratories at the University of Pennsylvania, shown on the following pages.

The great factory buildings of Fall River, Massachusetts, dominate the landscape like horizontal skyscrapers. As they represent the finest achievement of nineteenth-century American architecture, José Luis Sert's Married Student Housing on the following pages represents the epitome of American architecture today. Like the important building it is, it owes a debt to all great architecture, classical and recent, primitive and sophisticated, from the world over, and to those architects who emigrated to America, bringing with them traditions and memories that could be translated and adapted for a new country.

FIRE LANE
NO PARKING